Wicken Fen

Cambridgeshire

THE NATIONAL TRUST

The First English Nature Reserve

Wicken Fen is now one of the most important surviving areas of wetland in western Europe. It has been managed traditionally for centuries by sedge-cutting and peat-digging, which have produced a unique fenland habitat rich in rare wildlife, particularly insects. 1000 species of moth and butterfly, 1000 species of beetle, almost 2000 different flies, 20 dragonflies, 29 mammals and over 200 species of bird have been recorded on the fen.

The heart of the place is Wicken Sedge Fen, on the north side of Wicken Lode, an area that has never been drained. This makes it a unique remnant of the once-extensive Great Fen of East Anglia, which is now largely given over to intensive arable farming. The reserve also covers areas on the south side of Wicken Lode, encompassing Adventurers' Fen, the Mere and Priory Farm (Baker's Fen). These have been drained and cultivated in the past, notably during the Second World War, but are now managed for nature conservation. The result is a patchwork of habitats, each attracting different populations of plants and animals, and each requiring a different approach.

In 1999 Wicken Fen National Nature Reserve celebrated its centenary as a National Trust property. It is one of Britain's oldest nature reserves, and the first to be acquired by the National Trust, which bought two acres on 1 May 1899 for £10. 100 years and another 56 separate acquisitions later, the reserve has expanded to over 360 hectares (900 acres), and it is still growing.

'My personal feeling about Wicken is a complicated one: a mixture of enjoyment of fenland plants and animals (both aesthetically and scientifically), glimpsing the past and sensing the passage of time, while all the time enjoying the great open fen landscape under its vast skies. Of course I have little vignettes of special memory. For example watching swallowtails emerging from their pupae, looking at Adventurers' Fen in 1940 knowing it was soon to be destroyed and more recently the enjoyment of being part of a very special endeavour to understand Wicken and conserve it. To me Wicken is the first English Nature Reserve, a very special wetland and the most famous fen.'

Dr Norman Moore – one of the founding fathers of nature conservation and a former Chair of the Wicken Committee

Kingfishers can be seen over the Mere or on Wicken Lode

One of the small ponds on Sedge Fen, with yellow flag and ragged robin in flower

A southern hawker dragonfly resting on a yellow flag iris

The Creation of the Fens

The 4th Earl of Bedford, who led the group of Gentlemen Adventurers in financing the 17th-century drainage of the Fens

Wicken in summer

The area known as the Fens lies between the uplands of Lincolnshire, Norfolk, Suffolk and Cambridgeshire. The Fens were formed around 5000 years ago, when sea levels rose, the drainage of the fenland basin deteriorated, and the area became waterlogged. The wildwood that covered the region before it was submerged still survives in places in the form of huge 'bog oaks'. The remains of dead plants did not decay completely in this flooded area, but accumulated as peat, known locally as 'turf'.

Most human activity was limited to the 'isles' of clay, such as Ely and Wicken village, and the dry chalky uplands on the eastern margins of the marshland, such as the villages of Burwell, Reach and Swaffham Prior to the south-east of Wicken. The wet fens, however, were important, as they provided food (fish and wildfowl), fuel (peat and sedge), building materials (peat and clay for bricks, sedge and reed for roofing) and animal food and bedding.

There has always been pressure from outsiders to drain the Fens, in order to control flooding and improve the area's agricultural potential. The Romans built the Car Dyke across the western edge of the Fens between Lincoln and Cambridge to channel away water from rivers that had naturally run across the Fens. They probably also constructed some of the network of waterways called lodes, including Reach and Wicken Lodes. However, after 200 years their farm settlements fell into decline, as sea water levels rose again. After the Norman Conquest, new banks were constructed; the 'Roman Bank', a 60-mile-long earthwork around the Wash, was remade and lasted for 500 years, protecting more than a million acres of land. By the 14th century, the Fens were the most prosperous part of rural England, their wealth deriving from the unique wet landscape and its products.

The greatest push to drain the Fens came in the 1600s, with outside land-owners, notably the Crown and the Earl of Bedford, wishing to make money from arable crops and improved grassland. Cornelius Vermuyden, a Dutch engineer,

devised an elaborate system of drains and river diversions, which included rerouting the River Ouse along the Old and New Bedford Rivers, dug in 1637 and 1651. The scheme was unpopular, as it infringed property rights and offered no compensation. The locals had to maintain the new works, for which they had not asked, and which damaged their livelihoods and the local ecology. As a result, there were popular uprisings, resistance and sabotage by the so-called 'Fen Tigers'.

Unfortunately, Vermuyden did not take account of the effect of peat shrinkage, which naturally occurs when fens are drained. As the peat shrank, land levels became lower and lower. Water now has to be pumped away, instead of draining naturally into rivers by gravity. Flooding can be contained to a certain extent, but there is still a danger of inundation when certain weather and tidal conditions prevail. The disastrous floods of 1947 and 1953 are still widely remembered in the Fens.

Ancient bog oaks, such as this one found at nearby Stretham, are reminders of the pre-history of the Fens

The First 100 Years as a Nature Reserve

Albert Houghton, one of several Wicken men who guided visiting collectors around the fen, shown here with an 'Eddystone Lighthouse' moth trap in 1894

The Barnes brothers harvesting sedge

The National Trust was only three months old, when Herbert Goss, a distinguished entomologist, suggested that it should consider saving Wicken Fen. Four years later, in 1899, the Trust purchased two acres from Goss's fellow entomologist, J.C. Moberley. More portions were bought and donated steadily over the years. One of the most important benefactors was G.H. Verrall, who bequeathed 97 hectares (239 acres) to the National Trust in 1911; his gift comprised parts of the Sedge Fen and St Edmund's Fen, and all of what is now known as Verrall's Fen.

Naturalists have been a constant presence at Wicken Fen throughout the years of National Trust ownership. Unlike most Trust properties, the fen is managed by a local committee, to provide the specialist knowledge required to maintain the site. The Local Committee for Management was first appointed in 1911, to manage the fen 'to the best interests of the naturalists and others and to the best financial advantage consistent with such interests'.

From 1914, the committee employed a 'Watcher' of the fen, G.W. Barnes, upgraded to the role of 'Keeper' in 1925. Keeper Barnes was joined by his three sons, Henry, William and Wilfred, who maintained the fen by traditional methods, as far as they could. The Barnes family worked at Wicken Fen for most of the century, Wilfred retiring only in 1987. The first management plan was drawn up in 1936, but an early attempt to restore open habitat by clearing bush lasted only a fortnight, as heavy rain brought the work to an end.

Only Henry Barnes and his father remained on the fen throughout the Second World War, and routine work suffered as a result. Adventurers' Fen was requisitioned by the War Department and re-drained for food production. However, the committee secretary, William Thorpe, prevented the draining of Sedge Fen and the use of the wider area as a bombing range. The National Trust regained control of Adventurers' Fen after the war, and promoted wildlife conservation once more.

Charles Mitchell was appointed as the first full-time Warden of the Fen in 1961. He concentrated on reinstating systematic cropping regimes and raising funds to purchase the power-operated tools that would make such a scheme possible. A new management plan was drawn up to stem deterioration of the fen. In order to re-establish open habitat that had been lost, large-scale volunteer work parties began removing scrub.

Wicken Fen has been important for developing research techniques, such as 'pollen analysis', which traces the history of an area's vegetation by examining pollen and plant remains preserved in peat. There is a close relationship between the staff of the fen and Cambridge University, which carries out research here and contributes towards the upkeep of the fen.

19th-century moth collectors, in front of a sedge stack

Habitats

Sedge Fields

Sedge hath its home   oftest in fen
groweth in water   woundeth grimly
blood draweth   from any man
that maketh any   grasp at it.

Saxon Runic Poem

Harvested at Wicken since at least 1419, the Great Fen saw-sedge (*Cladium mariscus*) is the plant which defines Wicken Sedge Fen. This crop was so valuable to the local people that they resisted drainage of the fen. It was the sedge fields that allowed a diversity of fen plants to flourish, which in turn supported a huge range of insects and other animals. This proved to be Wicken Fen's saving grace at the end of the 19th century. Just as the market value of sedge and peat collapsed, the Victorian interest in natural history, and in creating collections of specimens, reached its peak.

After most of the surrounding fenland had been drained, Wicken Sedge Fen became a mecca for entomologists and botanists. In the 1820s Charles Darwin is said to have been among the many who visited from the University of Cambridge. (He is known to have collected beetles from the bottom of sedge boats arriving in Cambridge.) The number of moth traps on the fen at night prompted one commentator to compare the sight to a city illuminated at night.

The naturalists proved ready buyers for land with declining agricultural value. They could see that, unless they preserved their valuable hunting ground, Wicken Sedge Fen too would be drained.

Sedge is harvested after three or four years' growth, by which time it has become tall, dense and dominant. More frequent cutting would weaken the sedge. This infrequent cutting also allows a wide variety of other rare water-dependent fenland plants such as the milk parsley and marsh pea to grow in the sedge fields.

Sedge, however, is vulnerable to the process of succession. Only the repeated cropping since the 15th century has prevented its natural replacement by scrub. National Trust ownership of the fen in the early 20th century coincided with a decline in the vegetation, and the covering of the fen by scrub. In 1900, only 7% of Sedge and Verrall's Fen was bushes and trees (carr); in 1997 carr represented 76% and sedge only 10%. Photographs taken around 1900 highlight this change in vegetation very clearly.

Sedge-cutting in Wicken Fen, Cambridgeshire: Early Morning; detail from the 1878 painting by Robert Walker Macbeth

Meadowsweet is a common plant of damp places

(*Below*) View across one of the sedge fields. The trees in the background have all grown since the start of the 20th century

Sedge Fields

Why have they declined?

- The management committee was only able to employ one 'Keeper', G.W. Barnes, and later his three sons, compared to the 50 or so local people who had formerly worked in the area. The amalgamation into larger fields of many small plots previously worked individually discouraged diversity.

- Early attempts to secure good breeding grounds for Montagu's harriers by leaving Verrall's Fen alone encouraged carr, which was not suitable for these rare birds of prey.

- The drying-out of the fen has also contributed to the decline of the classic fen wet habitats. The installation of the sluice and pump at Upware in the 1940s stopped winter flooding, and summer levels in the Lode have been much reduced by increased water abstraction to irrigate crops in the surrounding farmland.

Since the 1960s much effort has been expended on removing scrub. Only by relying heavily on volunteer labour has this been possible; young crew members of HMS *Ganges* were among the first organised work parties, and they not only cleared the fen, but also put up the 'Ganges Hut'. This has provided

basic dormitory-style accommodation for volunteers since 1965; in 2001 it was converted to a new lecture/class room, and a new accommodation building will be built in the near future.

The process of scrub clearance will be much accelerated as a result of £322,000 funding from the Heritage Lottery Fund grant. By 2005, over 60 hectares (150 acres) of scrub will have been reverted to open sedge and fen habitats, thanks to the purchase of a mechanical scrub remover and the employment of new team of estate workers.

Promoting the sedge fields again will restore the fen to how a visitor in 1900 would have seen and experienced it.

Look out for

- Milk parsley, flowering in July, in the sedge fields

- Marsh pea, flowering in June and July, a rare plant that is relatively easily seen at Wicken Fen, on the edges of the sedge fields

- Wardens and volunteers cutting and bundling sedge, July and August

- Stacks of sedge awaiting collection by thatchers, in Lode Lane

- Marsh harriers in summer and hen harriers in winter quartering the fields

Marsh pea, flowering with yellow loosestrife

Purple loosestrife in flower. The Tower Hide in the background gives views over both Sedge Fen, and across the Mere on Adventurers' Fen

Meadow thistle with comfrey

Fen Meadows

Many of the open areas of the fen are now dominated by 'litter' (or fen hay), a species-rich wet meadow community dominated by grasses and wild flowers. Litter was cut annually at Wicken from the late 19th century for use as hay, becoming a significant crop after the slump in the sedge market.

The litter fields are valuable for the wide range of invertebrates supported by the diversity of plants. There are in fact two types of litter vegetation, one rare community dominated by purple moor-grass and the other by grasses such as reed and small-reed species. The areas with purple moor-grass are less widespread, being concentrated mainly on the drove at the western edge of Sedge Fen near Drainers' Dyke, as it thrives only in areas that have not previously been invaded by scrub.

Sedge fields are easily converted to litter by increasing the frequency of cropping to once every two or three years. This can be readily seen at the Godwin Plots, on the north-west corner of Sedge Fen. These were established by Sir Harry Godwin in the 1920s as an experiment to determine what happens to plant communities under different cutting regimes. The sedge communities occur where the vegetation is cut every three or four years, whereas the fen meadow communities flourish where cutting is annual or biannual. These plots are a landmark in ecology, and Godwin's experiment is still carried out at the site, with plots which are cut every four, three or two years, and annually, alongside a plot which is never cut and has developed into scrub.

The litter fields are subdivided into small areas, and a complicated pattern of cutting is in place to promote diversity. Some plots are cut annually, some biennially, and others two years in three. There is also seasonal variation in the cutting to promote a great diversity of plant and animal life. The patchwork effect, which prevailed from the 17th century, when the fen was owned and worked by numerous people, created the diversity of flora and fauna. The management of the litter meadows is designed to restore this pattern.

Look out for

- Purple loosestrife, flowering from June to August

- Yellow loosestrife, flowering in July and August

- Marsh thistle, up to two metres tall, spiney, flowering from June to October

- Devil's bit scabious, in flower from June to October

- Snipe, which nest in the fen meadows

- Hen harriers and owls, hunting low for small rodents, in the winter

Snipe can be heard 'drumming' in the breeding season, as they vibrate their outer tail feathers in display flight

Early marsh orchid, commonly flesh-pink, but colours from white to a deep red-purple are found

Droves

Several of the paths across the fen (known as droves) may well follow the routes of tracks dating from the subdivision of the fen in 1666. Sedge Fen Drove is certainly at least 300 years old. Together with Gardiner's Drove, it provides access across the width of the Sedge Fen.

The droves are between five and ten metres wide, the central part mown for ease of access for visitors and fen staff, and wide borders either side, which are cut in the autumn to provide a short, species-rich sward. The obvious disturbance of trampling and machinery means that there are more short-growing plants than in the meadows. Plants such as spike-rushes and marsh arrowgrass grow here. There are places on some of the droves that are almost always wet – ideal for various species of sweet grass, as well as rare soldier flies and craneflies.

Common lizard, easily seen on warm summer days

Look out for

- Ragged-robin, flowering from May to August

- Early marsh and southern marsh orchids, flowering in June

- Yellow rattle, flowering in July. Listen to it rattle later in the year, traditionally when it is time to harvest

- Silverweed, a flat-growing member of the rose family, ideally suited to heavy traffic

- Common comfrey, abundant on the fen, and favoured by bumble-bees

- Common lizard, sunbathing on the boardwalk (a modern drove?)

Grass snakes can be seen basking on the banks of the ditches, as well as swimming. They are harmless, and the only snake found on the Fens

Water violets

Drainers' Dyke

Lodes, Ditches and Drains

Wicken Lode, which divides the reserve, is one of a number of ancient manmade waterways in the South Cambridgeshire Fens. These run from fen-edge villages on the chalk upland to the River Cam, providing navigable water access across the fens both to the sea and to major markets such as Cambridge. Monk's Lode from Newmarket meets Wicken Lode; Burwell Lode forms the eastern boundary of the Adventurers' Fen side of the reserve, running from Burwell to the Cam at Upware.

The lodes carry drainage water from the ditches and drains that criss-cross the fens. While the water in Wicken Lode is slightly below the land surface of the Sedge Fen, it is above the level of the drained Adventurers' Fen. All the other lodes in the area are several metres above the drained farmland. Waterproof banks have been built up to help keep the fen wet and to prevent the adjacent agricultural fields from flooding. The water in Monk's and Wicken Lodes is of very high quality, supporting a rich diversity of flora and fauna.

Look out for

*   Kingfishers

*   Mute swans. Their large nests are unmistakable

*   Reed warblers, nesting and acting as unwitting parents to cuckoo chicks

*   Yellow and white water lilies, water mint, arrowhead, with different shaped leaves above and below the water, and hornwort, completely submerged

*   Fish. Many different species, including bitterling, which lay their eggs in freshwater mussels

A network of ditches and smaller drains dissects Sedge Fen. The oldest of these is probably Drainers' Dyke, dug in the 17th century. Running from Spinney Bank down to Wicken Lode, it cuts between Sedge and Verrall's Fens.

As well as acting as drainage channels, the dykes provided access to individual plots of sedge and peat diggings for the villagers, and served as boundary markers. As the pattern of ownership changed and the cutting of sedge declined, the dykes were not used so regularly, and many became choked by vegetation and dried up. These are now left as damp depressions in the ground.

Each stage in the life of a ditch favours particular species. Dragonflies prefer open water, whilst reed warblers favour reed-fringed ditches; water rail like a ditch when only a narrow shallow channel of water remains. The ditches are therefore cleared regularly, but not all simultaneously, providing different habitats from one ditch to the next. Some kinds of slubbing (as ditch clearance is called) are done only every twelve years.

Look out for

- Grass snakes swimming in hot weather

- Many species of dragonfly and damselfly, including emerald damselfly (July to September), red-eyed damselfly (May to August), southern hawker dragonfly (July to September), ruddy darter (July and August)

- Hairy dragonfly, a recent return to Wicken Fen as a result of improved ditch management, but nationally a rare species (May and June)

- Variable damselfly, again nationally rare, but a common species on the fen (June and July)

- Stoneworts, in the dyke alongside Gardiner's Drove

- Greater bladderwort, Wicken's only carnivorous plant, each one eating up to a quarter of a million invertebrates annually

Mute swans with cygnets on Wicken Lode

An adult reed warbler feeds a cuckoo chick. The nest is built around reed stems

Tawny owls are the commonest of the five owl species regularly seen at Wicken Fen

(*Below*) Brimstone butterflies can over-winter and are one of the first butterflies to be seen each spring

(*Opposite*) The woodland floor. The sedge, still with a foothold under the trees, will reassert itself if the fen becomes wetter, or the scrub is cleared

Carr and Woodland

Although too much scrub and woodland damages the classic fen habitat, in a county with relatively few trees it is in itself also a valuable habitat. The ground is too wet to support large old trees, but in some areas birch and, to a lesser extent, ash, oak and alder have grown up through the carr (bushes and small trees up to five metres tall). Given time and no management, these trees would develop into woodland, as at Holme Fen. Although this site is also an undrained area in the fens, it differs significantly from Wicken Fen, being the largest birch wood in the country, with no open vistas. The wooded area near to the Brickpits, where the gault clay rises close to the surface, has existed since the early 19th century. The main woody species in the areas of carr are alder buckthorn, common buckthorn and willows, plus guelder rose and hawthorn. There are apple trees near the sites of former brick workers' cottages.

The spread of carr is a relatively recent phenomenon. Alder buckthorn was not recorded at all at Wicken Fen until 1861, but by the end of the 19th century it was said to have been abundant, the seeds spread by birds which were fond of its berries. Bushes became established with

reduced sedge-cutting, and seemed to grow best on the ridges of peat workings, rather than in the furrows which flooded in winter. Once established, impenetrable thickets soon develop, with the crowns forming a closed canopy.

Most of the plants characteristic of sedge and litter communities do not survive in the thick carr areas, although some other plants do well, such as marsh fern, mosses and liverworts, and fen nettle. The variety of ferns is increasing, as more characteristic woodland ferns are appearing. Similarly, the list of mosses and lichens is now much longer than in the mid-20th century. Birds and insects are commoner on the edges of new carr than in areas of old carr.

Look out for

- Flocks of fieldfares, feeding on alder buckthorn berries, September

- Guelder rose, actually a type of honeysuckle, white flowers in June, red berry clusters through the winter

- Brimstone butterflies, both alder and common buckthorn are food plants

- Woodcock, woodpeckers and owls

Listen out for

- Nightingales singing

- Woodpeckers tapping

Adventurers' Fen, the Mere and the Reed-beds

Marsh harriers are regular summer visitors. Watch out for males passing food mid-air to the females, who do not allow the males near to a nest with young in it

(*Below right*) Wardens harvesting reed

(*Opposite*) Common reed (*Phragmites australis*) in winter, ready for harvesting

The 'Adventurers', speculators who financed drainage schemes in return for land, claimed the area south of Wicken Lode, towards Burwell Lode, in 1636. However, the area was not finally drained until 1840, after which the land was given over first to agriculture, and then to large-scale digging of turf (peat). By the end of the 19th century, the level of the land had sunk so far that several windpumps were needed to keep the turf-pits drained. When the turf industry collapsed, the drainage ceased, and water, reeds and wildfowl reclaimed the low-lying land.

During the Second World War Adventurers' Fen was once more cleared and drained for food production, as part of the 'Dig for Victory' campaign. The horticulturalist Alan Bloom carried out this work, and documented it in his book *Farm in the Fen* and in a 1941 film, which includes extraordinary footage of massive bog oaks being blown up. After the war, however, the land was returned to the National Trust, and was allowed to revert to wet meadows and reed-beds.

The Mere was excavated from 1952 to 1955, and further wet scrapes on Brett's and Trevelyan's Pieces were developed from 1992, specifically to encourage wildfowl. These are home to a diverse range of birds in the winter months. Baker's Fen, bought in 1993, is being restored to wet pasture from arable land; it is still often referred to as Priory Farm. Wintering, migrant and breeding birds all now use the area.

The reed-beds on Adventurers' Fen are among the most extensive inland examples in Britain, and therefore a valuable habitat, especially as coastal areas come under increasing threat from rising sea levels. Reed-beds are host to many insects, but do not favour a wide variety of plants.

Reed is harvested at Wicken in late January–early February. About 60% of the reed-beds are cut on a four-year cycle. This does not produce the best-quality thatching reed, but is far more beneficial for wildlife than an annual cut. The reed-leopard moth, for instance, has a two-year maturation inside the reed stem before it appears. However, about 15% of the reed is still managed for annual cutting, and is sold to local thatchers. The reed-beds are flooded after cutting to encourage strong new growth; regular cutting is essential to prevent the drying out of the reed-beds and invasion by other plant species. The remaining reed-beds on the reserve are located on Verrall's Fen, and are not cut at all, as the area is currently far too wet to manage.

Look out for

- Lapwing, on the wet grasslands, all year, but large flocks in winter

- Wigeon, teal, shoveler, on the Mere, large numbers in winter

- Bittern, over winter, and bearded tits in the reeds around the Mere, most months

- Cormorants, on the island trees in the Mere, all year

- Marsh harriers, during the summer months

Fenman's Cottage and Settlement

'The Lode' (now Lode Lane) was a thriving hamlet with a separate identity to the rest of Wicken village, as the livelihoods of its inhabitants were closely tied to the fen. They relied upon the traditional harvesting of sedge, reed, litter and buckthorn (which was used in making gunpowder), digging peat and clay, and the shooting and trapping of wildfowl, eels and fish. They were also responsible for transporting these fen goods to market via the lode and river network.

The cottage at 5 Lode Lane, opposite the William Thorpe Building, is a surviving example of the local style of building. It was built in various stages between the early 18th and early 20th centuries, the oldest part being the thatched end. The pantiled section was probably added to house a second family; the small bedroom at the back is the newest addition. Between 1924 and 1972 the cottage was occupied by Reggie Butcher and his mother Alice. Reggie was disabled and unable to work on the fen, but he made a living by selling household items, hatching eggs, making fretwork items and issuing fishing licences. Male members of previous generations had been turf-cutters and labourers on the fen – Reggie's great-uncle ran his own turf-cutting business in the lane.

The cottage was acquired in 1974 by the National Trust, which restored it using traditional materials and methods between 1988 and 1990, and opened it to the public in 1990. It is furnished as it might have been at the start of the 20th century. The same local building materials would have been used in earlier fen 'hovels', which were traditionally constructed on wooden piles driven into the peat, or on mattresses of reeds and osiers. With willow and sedge roofs, and walls of clay-bats lined with sun-dried turf-blocks, they were flexible structures suited to the marshy ground on which they stood.

Look out for

- Peat blocks, sun-dried and used like bricks, protected from the rain by lime plaster

- Local gault clay, used for bricks, floors and roofing pantiles; also as an ingredient in daub, plaster and limewash, this underlies the fen. There are flooded brick pits and the remains of a brick kiln to be seen on the reserve

- Reed bundles, used as infill material in the walls, for the thatched roof, and as a base for ceiling plasters

- Sedge, added to daub and plasters, and used for the thatched ridge of the cottage, as well as the thatch of the shed

Residents of 'the Lode', about 1905

(*Opposite*) Interior of the cottage, looking from what was originally a dairy, through to the 'backhouse' kitchen. The floor bricks are made of local gault clay

(*Below*) Looking up the lane, about 1910. The cottage on the right is no. 5, then owned by George Butcher, Alice's father-in-law

Working in the Fens

The windpump

(*Below right*) Boats loaded with turf blocks and sedge waiting to be unloaded at the end of Wicken Lode

(*Opposite*) Reed bundles are transported by boat from the reed beds on Adventurers' Fen to the end of Wicken Lode, where they are stacked for collection by thatchers

The Fen staff still uses the Lode to get around, in a fen boat of traditional design (albeit motorised), which is kept in the open reed-thatched boathouse at the end of Wicken Lode. Traditional fen boats, between 6 and 7.5 metres long and about 2 metres wide, or fen lighters, which were between 12 and 15 metres long, were of shallow draft to be able to work in low water levels. These were unique cargo-carrying boats, made from wood, flat-bottomed and rounded at the bow and stern; their design harked back to the Vikings. They were mostly pulled by horse or donkey, or used a single square sail, and were often worked in gangs. A horse-drawn gang of three transported sedge and turf along Wicken Lode until the 1940s.

Further evidence of human intervention in the environment can be seen at the start of the walks on the Sedge Fen. Before the advent of steam and diesel pumping engines, wind power was used to drain the peat pits and fields. The windpump, originally located near Harrison's Drove on the edge of Adventurers' Fen, was one of six in use here in the late 19th century. The windpump had fallen into a state of disrepair by 1956, when it was dismantled, moved and restored. Further conservation was carried out in 1988 to return it to working order. The windpump at Wicken Fen is now the only one out of thousands that used to exist still operating in the Fens. It is now set up to pump water from the ditch on to the land, but, ironically, is not often started up, as it floods the visitor route!

Evidence of the local brick industry can also be seen from the walks on the Sedge Fen, in the area known as Little Breed Fen. There is a complex of brickpits along the eastern boundary of Sedge Fen, where the peat gives way to clay on the fen edge. Before the brick workings were developed here, the area was listed in the 1842 Tithe Award as a mixture of grass, arable and woodland – quite distinct from the fen habitat. In 1869 a plot was bought by John Owers, a brick-maker from nearby Soham. By 1880 there was a brickyard in full operation, with a kiln and a windpump to keep the pits dry. The yard was still operational in 1894, but by 1901 was no longer in use. The remains of the kiln can still be seen. The brickpits have long since filled with water and are now an important open area of freshwater for wildlife. The sites of vanished brickworkers' cottages, on Sedge Fen Drove as it enters Little Breed Fen, are revealed by the plants that grew in their gardens – snowdrops, for instance, as well as fruit trees.

Ebbing and Flowing Biodiversity

Swallowtail butterfly. The biggest of British butterflies was once a common sight in July, but unfortunately is no longer seen at Wicken Fen

Wicken Fen survives today because Victorian naturalists recognised its importance as a refuge for rare fenland flora and fauna in a dry and intensively farmed landscape. Due to their efforts and those of many naturalists since, the fen has one of the longest species lists of any reserve in Britain. The list is far from complete – some groups have hardly been studied – but it includes more than 2,000 species of two-winged flies, 1,000 species of beetles and 1,000 species of moths, 212 species of spiders and nearly 300 species of vascular plants.

The rate of extinction from Wicken Fen is a cause for alarm, however. Some species are becoming more vulnerable and even disappearing, for a number of reasons, including lack of water, the changing acidity of the soil, isolation from other fens, and the loss of open habitat. In a few cases, such as the beetles *Oberea oculata* and *Panagaeus crux-major*, it is hoped that determined searching may reveal small hidden populations.

No longer present at Wicken Fen

- Swallowtail butterfly, the iconic species of Wicken, has become extinct here, despite several carefully controlled re-introductions to the reserve. Its caterpillars' sole food plant, the milk parsley, has performed poorly because of the past drying-out of the fen. Work to improve the sedge fields should increase and safeguard the milk parsley population – and in the long term make Wicken a viable site for the swallowtail once more. Currently, all the British sites for swallowtails are in the Norfolk Broads, where the type of habitat favoured by the species is protected by being surrounded by miles of similar marsh.

- Fen orchid, the last of which was recorded in 1945. Its decline is the result of both over-enthusiastic specimen-collecting, and the end of peat-digging, which had provided suitable 'open' habitat.

- Water voles, increasingly threatened nationally, have presumably disappeared from the reserve due to the presence of mink

- Montagu's harrier, due to loss of open fen habitat

- Common hawker dragonfly, one of several species associated with the acidic conditions generated by turf-digging

- Various moths, including reed tussock, marsh dagger, many-lined and gypsy moth

- White-clawed crayfish

Bitterns currently spend the winter in the reed beds at Wicken Fen. None has bred in the area since the 1930s, but it is hoped the expansion of the reed beds will encourage them to return to breed

Very rare species still present at Wicken Fen

Fen violet, colonies of which have been located in cleared areas on Verrall's Fen

Fen violet was recorded by C.C. Babington in his *Flora of Cambridgeshire* (1860) as one of the species that 'most abound' at Wicken. By the end of the 19th century it was only rarely seen, and by the 1920s considered extinct at Wicken Fen. However, in 1980, a seedling was spotted in peat soil samples that had been taken from beneath scrub on the fen. It developed into a fully-grown plant at the Cambridge University Botanic Garden. In 1982 a large flowering population was discovered on Verrall's Fen – and this population has been closely monitored ever since. The fen violet appears to flourish particularly in recently cleared areas, when the peat is laid bare. After two seasons, other plants will have been spread into the area, and the violets eliminated once more. The abundance noticed by Babington were probably the result of the peat diggings, the decline of which led to the decline of the fen violet. Long-lived seeds are the plant's way of competing with other species that are more dominant in the short term, and ensuring its long-term survival.

Fen ragwort is now present at Wicken Fen in small, carefully monitored and managed numbers. It was recorded in the early 19th century almost exclusively in the fenland around Ely, but no reliable records exist for after 1857. However, in 1972 it was rediscovered growing in a ditch in the area. In 1991 seed was collected and grown on in cultivation, and in 1992 50 seedlings were planted out in varying positions on the edge of one of the ponds on Sedge Fen. Those plants in the wettest conditions thrived the best – slugs attacked the others, but obviously did not enjoy the pond margin conditions. The fen ragwort is surviving at Wicken Fen, but its future elsewhere in the surrounding countryside is doubtful. If Wicken Fen is enlarged, however, it is one of the vulnerable species that may well benefit.

Bittern, under extreme pressure nationally, with very few birds breeding in this country, have been present at Wicken Fen in most recent winters, when one or two birds have been recorded. Before the drainage of Adventurers' Fen, between Wicken and Burwell, there were breeding pairs in the area, as the habitat was then ideal for them. The last record for breeding is from 1937. With coastal reed-beds under threat from rising sea-levels, the programme of extending and improving the reed-beds at Wicken Fen has been funded by the European Union LIFE Bittern Project, and by the Heritage Lottery Fund as part of the Centenary Project (see p.30). It is hoped that continued improvement in the habitat may lead to a pair of bitterns breeding here.

Increasingly common species

The changing landscape of the fen has benefited other species that would not previously have been comfortable here. Drier conditions, more trees and bushes, and changing acidity have benefited the following species, all new to the reserve since 1950. Some species are increasing their range generally:

- Woodcock, nightingale

- Emperor dragonfly and black-tailed skimmer

- Red deer, muntjac and Chinese water deer

- Brown argus butterfly

- Roesel's bush-cricket, long-winged conehead

- Lady-fern, male-fern, narrow buckler-fern

Long-winged coneheads were first recorded at Wicken Fen in the late 1990s. Previously only found in the southern counties of England, it has been steadily expanding its range northwards, presumably due to climate change

The Centenary Project

Children make full use of Wicken Fen's resources via special events and organised educational trips. Minibeast hunting (above) and pond dipping are favourite activities in the adapted education area

The celebration of the reserve's centenary in 1999 provided an opportunity for looking to the long-term future of Wicken Fen and for raising substantial sums to fund major conservation projects. The Local Management Committee and National Trust staff created a Centenary Project, outlining four main areas of work for 2000–5, and costing around £1 million. It aims to restore Wicken Fen to its wetland glory and secure its future. The Heritage Lottery Fund has contributed substantially towards this project. The main parts of the Centenary Project are:

The Restoration of the Sedge Fen and Verrall's Fen

The remaining open areas are immensely valuable, both for the conservation of rare habitat, particularly purple moor-grass litter and sedge fields, and for reasons of historical continuity. Five centuries of sedge-cutting constitute a remarkable record of sustained management for one crop, and continuity of one vegetation type. That the Sedge Fen has never been grazed but always mown sets Wicken apart from all other surviving fen fragments in this country and contributes to the distinctiveness of Wicken's flora and fauna.

The clearance of scrub and restoration of large areas of mown fen have therefore become the main aims in the future management of the fen. It is hoped to reinstate litter and sedge fields in the centre of the Sedge Fen, perhaps by restoring a pattern of strips. Water supply to the centre of the fen will also be improved by reopening some long-lost ditches.

The first step will be to remove 54 hectares of scrub. A new mechanical digger and a team of new workers will make the clearance task much quicker and the work more thorough than previous attempts at scrub removal. The plan does, however, leave over 60 hectares of scrub, for the benefit of those species, such as ferns, which have taken advantage of the trend towards scrub in the 20th century.

The project will result in a great increase in the area of Sedge Fen requiring regular management and cropping. As there will also be over 40 hectares on Verrall's Fen newly cleared, a radical departure from current practices will be instituted. A small number of semi-wild Konig ponies have been introduced to graze. The ponies are the nearest living equivalent to the original European wild horse, and are suited to wet conditions. The vegetation that develops will be closely monitored, as it will probably differ significantly from mown meadows.

New Reed-beds on Adventurers' Fen

Forty hectares in the south-eastern corner of the reserve will be released from deep drainage and, because the land is low-lying and carried extensive reed-beds before drainage, we plan to re-create a wet reed-bed. This part of the project will be carried out as part of the National Trust's contribution to the UK Biodiversity Action Plan for reed-beds. It is an extension of the work begun in 1996 to restore the existing reed-beds as part of the EU LIFE Bittern Project.

Biological Records Centre and Archive

The archive and biological records of the fen represent an extremely valuable asset. At the moment, no dedicated space is available for storing this material, which remains dispersed among a number of

Otters returned to Wicken Fen in 1999, after an absence of 60 years. The habitat here is ideal for them, although the visitor is more likely to see tracks and spraint (droppings) than the animal itself

recorders, and in original papers and manuscripts. In their present form, these records are all but inaccessible to those who work at the fen and others who wish to study them. The Centenary Project includes a plan to computerise all 100,000 biological records and to house the archive at the fen.

Improvements for Visitors

To meet the needs of the many different groups who visit Wicken Fen, there are various projects underway. With funding from WREN, the education room has moved into the Ganges Hut, to provide a larger classroom space. A new residential centre will be built for volunteers. The boardwalk is gradually being replaced with recycled plastic, as the hardwood used initially has decayed quickly in the wet peat. A new Tower Hide has been erected to give views over Verrall's Fen, a good vantage point for seeing both Hen and Marsh harriers, as well as the Konig ponies.

Konig ponies grazing Verrall's Fen, helping reserve staff to keep scrub from encroaching on recently cleared areas

The Next 100 Years

This aerial photo shows clearly the wetland reserve surrounded by large intensively farmed fields

Wicken Fen is an isolated reserve surrounded by intensive agriculture, and so any pressure on plants and animals needing wetter conditions and a specialised habitat is liable to have severe consequences. Unseasonal flooding or drought could easily cause the extinction of a vulnerable species on the reserve.

With Wicken Fen's centenary, a new vision took shape. The National Trust plans a significant expansion of Wicken Fen over the next 100 years. This will mean acquiring drained farmland between Wicken and the edge of the Fens along the chalk ridge villages, and managing it for wildlife. When pumping ceases, the land will become wetter. This will encourage a wildlife and fen landscape recognisable to Eric Ennion, who wrote a classic account of Adventurers' Fen in 1942.

The vision is for a truly large-scale lowland nature reserve, with a network of walks and cycleways to benefit the growing population of Cambridgeshire as much as the wildlife. Increased pressure for housing and roads has resulted in the loss of many previously green areas. Consequently, people looking for peaceful walking, cycling and enjoyment of the countryside have to travel longer distances to reach the pockets of open space that remain. The vision for the future of Wicken Fen would go some way to counteract this trend in the local area.

Why expand Wicken Fen?

- Wicken Fen is an internationally important wetland, but it is currently too small and too isolated to be sustainable

- Creating a large new reserve around Wicken Fen will lower extinction rates

- It will improve Cambridgeshire's currently poor biodiversity, helping the county deliver its targets in the UK Biodiversity Action Plan

- In the project area, land drainage is unsustainable in the longer term and peat/soil loss will make farming uneconomic. The creation of a large new wetland reserve is an ideal alternative land use

- Cambridgeshire is an ideal place to create new habitats to make up for the loss of internationally important wetlands on the coast because of the rise in sea levels

- It will provide new recreational opportunities and many other benefits for residents and visitors